ENTERTAINING THOUGHTS

ALTON DOUGLAS

To Lesley
Cheers!
Alton Douglas

BREWIN BOOKS

First published by
Brewin Books Ltd, 56 Alcester Road,
Studley, Warwickshire B80 7LG in 2016
www.brewinbooks.com

ISBN: 978-1-85858-554-3

The moral right of the author has been asserted.

A Cataloguing in Publication Record
for this title is available from the British Library.

Typeset in Galliard.
Printed in Great Britain by
Bell & Bain Ltd.

ACKNOWLEDGEMENTS

In this, my third anecdotal book, I would like to thank my friends without whose help it would all have been possible. Duty (and a relentless publisher) forces me to acknowledge contributions from Keith Ackrill, Neil Allen, Alan Brewin (my relentless publisher), Johnny Hillyard, Sharon Jones, Dave Kilner, the late Bill McGuffie, Dennis Moore, Alec Owen, Bob Sterling, Bryan Summerfield and Ken Windsor. Having always jotted down interesting tales the rest of this collection is down to me – so far my attempts at blackmail have proved unsuccessful.

The success of "The Original Alton Douglas", "I Forgot To Tell You" and "Laughs In The Right Place", are ongoing so I won't bang on too long except to say that if you have not purchased them – shame on you!

Once again there are humorous and unusual stories with just a hint that I may be a bit of a drama queen.

Finally, I must remember to thank Jo whose contribution has been inexplicable.

Any errors are entirely due to a breakdown in communication somewhere along the lines.

In the 70s I appeared in a BBC TV programme called "The Knockers", during the course of which I "knocked" the Entertainment Secretaries from our local working men's clubs. One of their duties was to write reviews of their shows. I remember them as being roughly like this:

I complained to the agent that he keeps booking the same acts. He said, "Why don't you keep the acts and change the audience?" I think he meant it.

We had to cancel the talent contest as there were no entrants. Still, it could have been worse.

The committee thought it was time to book a piano tuner but I told them to forget it unless he could sing as well.

I was pleased to help the girl singer out of her dress but her lawyer said she was trying to get into it.

By the way, there is some good news following the darts competition. The hospital reckon they can save the Chairman's eye.

I tried to give the ventriloquist some advice. I might just as well have talked to myself.

I must admit that I enjoyed the female impersonator as much as the next man.

The 50s pop singer was very good. It was just a shame that none of his fan club could manage our stairs.

I warned them to observe silence during the Bingo. If they want to make a racket they should wait until the acts are on.

Someone suggested that we needed a piper for Burns Night so I have booked one for November 5th.

Due to a lack of funds we had to stipulate that this year's Father Xmas should be someone of portly build, preferably with their own whiskers. We would like to thank Maureen Smethurst for volunteering.

The magician's first spot was not up to standard. I told him that I hoped he had something better up his sleeve.

I don't know why a high-wire walker would attempt his act in a single storey club with a low roof. I should think he must be brain-dead.

He assured me that their romantic duets were much better since the divorce.

The Glenn Miller Tribute Band were very well received but I felt that they should have played more of his recent hits.

He wore a blindfold and threw daggers at his assistant. I said to him, "Call yourself an act? I could do that with my eyes shut."

We will be holding our annual "Sink a Yard of Ale" contest next month although I know it's not everyone's cup of tea.

Following complaints that committee members seemed to be winning a large percentage of raffle prizes an emergency meeting was held. The committee confirmed that they were perfectly satisfied with the current system. At the same time they announced that, at the earliest opportunity, they would be holding a car boot sale.

I booked him because the contract said he was a tenor but when I went to pay him he said it was not enough.

"TELLING TALES"

When I appeared in Blackpool, in 1968, my landlady could really have out-rivalled Sheridan's Mrs Malaprop. After I had stopped laughing I used to jot down her comments:

"I never speak ill of the deaf."

She came back from a neighbour's funeral and I asked, "Was it a burial?" "Oh, yes," she replied, "I can't stand them creations."

"He said their relatives were really effluent."

A visit to the doctors produced this: "I'm not going there again. He wanted me to have one of those infernal examinations."

Above all I've always treasured one line that was more Spike Milligan than Mrs Malaprop: "We'll have a chicken on Sunday so all three of us can have a leg."

✳   ✳   ✳   ✳

Billy Forrest, the Sutton Coldfield agent, was someone who had a problem with his own native language. He rang me once, " 'ere I've just read your biography. I wonder if you could help me with my memos." On another occasion he said, to one of his acts, "You won't recognise my car when you see it. I've had it dyed."

✳   ✳   ✳   ✳

Talking to an act about an agent we both worked for I said, "He never acknowledges the commission I send him." He replied, "You know why? He resents you having the other 90%."

✳   ✳   ✳   ✳

Speaking of that agent someone said, "If you were in your coffin he'd try and claim the brass handles."

✳   ✳   ✳   ✳

It was said of the Birmingham agent Dave Kenton, that if you rang him after the football results, any Saturday, somehow he could find you a booking for that night. If you were working for him that night, and you rang during the football results, he would cancel your booking.

Actor, Charlie Hall, was born in Ward End, in Birmingham and appeared in almost 50 films with Laurel and Hardy (my personal favourite is Charlie as the proprietor next door in "Tit for Tat"). During a break in filming he returned home to his mother's in England. She refused to wash his socks! Now, you have to remember that in the 30s and 40s men's socks were either black or a dull grey. Charlie had bought his in America where socks could be any colour from green to vermilion. His mother, conscious of the neighbours, flatly refused to put them on the washing line.

* * * *

I performed, in cabaret, at the Dorchester Hotel. It was a small private party and in the audience were film producer, Otto Preminger, Marlene Dietrich, Richard Burton and Elizabeth Taylor. The other artistes appearing with me were those fine comedy acrobats, Ted and Hilda Durante. Strangely, I don't remember much about the evening except that half way through my spot Richard Burton fell asleep. Because the hotel management had failed to provide us with a changing room I had to use the gent's toilet. When I went back afterwards someone had stolen one of my socks.

* * * *

The 60s were still quite a naïve age. They were for me, anyway. So, when someone told me that a certain female xylophonist had a foot fetish I had to reach for my Harold Robbins'. It seemed she had a predilection for toe-sucking – not theirs. I asked her boyfriend, "I can't imagine sucking anyone's toes, what's it like?" He grimaced at me, "I suppose it depends on how much you like the taste of wool."

Comedy magician, Murray Smith, finished his spot in a working men's club, in the North and walked over to the bar for his customary soft drink. A burly character said to him, "That was very good, lad but you want to forget the comedy and stick to the magic." Murray replied, "Thank you very much for your advice. By the way, what do you do for a living?" "I'm a long-distance lorry driver." Murray looked at him, "I've always said if you want a concise, unbiased, show business critique always go to a f—— long-distance lorry driver."

✻ ✻ ✻ ✻

Booked for a show, at the New Theatre, in Hull, with a less than popular star, I received a call that very morning to say that it was cancelled because they had sold so few tickets. The manager said it was perfectly alright as he knew the couple personally.

✻ ✻ ✻ ✻

My billing on one occasion read, "Alton Douglas – laughs with a trombone." They must have heard my playing.

✻ ✻ ✻ ✻

Ronnie Dukes and Ricki Lee performed a frantic act. Along with their backing group they became one of the biggest attractions in clubland, in the 70s. Ronnie was a little butterball of a man who worked at a frenetic pace and came off, after an hour's performing, literally soaked from head to toe with perspiration. At one venue we were walking along the corridor afterwards and met a disc jockey who had been appearing in an adjoining room. Seeing Ronnie the DJ (remember this is a man who plays records for a living) said to him, "I can sympathize with you. I've just done a really hectic session."

Ronnie hit him.

I appeared in cabaret, for a week, at Bishop's Waltham Country Club. It was run by two gentle men, in fact, on my first night, to their great amusement, I re-christened it Queen's Waltham Country Club. Although they were obviously very fond of each other there was an element of competition, minor disagreements of who should do what. I walked into the kitchen one day and asked the sole occupant, "All right, where is he today?" There was a pause and then, with an air of supreme triumph, he declared, "I'm ironing, her's coal."

* * * *

George Bartram, who was my publicist and agent for several years, could be said to have certain eccentricities. He invited us to have a look around his new home in Barnt Green – and we did. Through the downstairs windows in turn without once setting foot inside.

* * * *

Nottingham comedian, Alec Owen, spent an afternoon at Chepstow Races with the popular singer, Frankie Vaughan. As they walked in the gatekeeper waved Frankie through but refused to do the same with the slightly lesser-known Alec. Now, I should tell you that Alec was almost, at that time, as wide as he was high. Frankie, realising he was alone, turned round and saw this corpulent figure looking crestfallen. He called out, "Let him in, he's alright, he's my jockey."

* * * *

I was once accused, by a viewer, of using a racist joke on a television programme. Childish maybe but racist? I'll let you judge for yourself:

Two boys meet in the street. One of them, out with his family, is wearing a turban. The other one asks, "Are you Sikhs?" "No, I'm seven."

In the late 80s I played the part of Larry, a ventriloquist who was dying of TB, in the BBC radio play, "Troupers". I spent the whole of the morning hacking and spluttering my way through my lines. In theatrical terms, if you played a small part, it was always known as "a cough and a spit". This must have been one of the few times when someone playing a leading part, could literally say they had "a cough and a spit".

✳ ✳ ✳ ✳

When I was a guest on Pete Murray's "Open House" I was telling him beforehand, how nerve-wracking it was for me, a virtually unknown comedian, to appear on a major BBC radio programme. He reassured me by telling me that the previous week his guest had been the very experienced actor, Wilfred Brambell (from "Steptoe and Son") and he was so terrified that when he got up to leave there were two pools of water on the table where his hands had been.

✳ ✳ ✳ ✳

A friend of mine started work, as a young man, at the BBC. His first job was on a weather programme. In those days the weatherman, or woman, would describe the conditions and an off-screen assistant, using a pointer, would indicate each area. On his first day, as pointer man, due to his nervousness, the pointer danced all over the screen so that Birmingham could have been anywhere from Blackpool to The Wash. After a few seconds of this the producer screamed out, "For God sake get me someone who doesn't suffer from D.T's."

✳ ✳ ✳ ✳

Bob Sterling tells of the man who claimed to be a member of the orchestra that played "Tchaikovsky's 1812 Overture". Someone asked what instrument he played and he replied, "The cannon."

Retired acrobat, Bob, also remembered this one:

When a plague of flying-ants caused the performance to end prematurely at a variety theatre in the Australian outback, the manager cabled a message to his agent, "Show stopped by flying ants." By return came, "Book 'em for another week!"

*   *   *   *

Tony Mercer, who topped the bill during our summer season at Weston-Super-Mare, in 1970, told me a nice tale. If you remember he was one of the lead singers with "The Black and White Minstrels". For several years Tony would mainly croon ballads and his friend, Dai Francis, did an act as Al Jolson. One night Tony was cornered at the door of the Victoria Palace by a woman who asked for his autograph. She said, "You were very good but my husband can sing all those songs better than Dai Francis, I'd even go so far as to say that he's better than the real Alf Johnson."

*   *   *   *

Johnny Hillyard, the hypnotist, told me about a musician who was in hospital for a minor operation. The conversation with the anaesthetist went like this:

"Would you like to listen to some music while you drift off?"

"That would be nice. What have you got?"

"The Bee Gees?"

"No thanks – I'm a jazz musician."

"I've got just the thing. How about Acker Bilk?"

Pause. "Could I have an extra injection please?"

*   *   *   *

I worked on several occasions, with The Krankies. Their real surname was Tough and Ian told me that the family had a butcher's shop in Clydebank. Their slogan was, "If it's Tough's, it's tender."

In my days as a warm-up comedian with the television programme, "The Golden Shot", I would often invite the guest artistes back to our flat afterwards. Being away from home so often, myself, I knew what it was like to stare at hotel room walls for an evening. Amongst those who took up the invitation were Bill Maynard, George Truzzi and one of my all-time favourites the Scottish comic, Chic Murray. A couple of years later, when I was appearing in "The Anita Harris Show" for three weeks at the King's Theatre in Glasgow, Chic came backstage. He remembered that night, "You invited me back to your flat and we had a very pleasant evening. I met your lovely wife, a wonderful person. How is he?"

✳   ✳   ✳   ✳

After I unexpectedly compered "The Golden Shot", in 1973, when Norman Vaughan was taken ill, it seemed that virtually the whole nation had been watching on that Sunday afternoon. Afterwards, for several weeks, I seemed to be recognised by almost everyone I met. I discovered then how much I resented the recognition part of show business and that fame wasn't for me. I found the transition from unknown to the opposite very embarrassing. So much so that, after a few days, I became quite belligerent with everyone. This was one exchange in a motorway service station:

"You're the bloke from – "

"That's right."

"You were on that – "

"That's right."

"You did the – "

"That's right."

"Hey, Mavis. Look who we've got here! It's that nice Les Dennis."

As I walked away I heard Mavis mutter, "Seemed like a miserable old git to me."

My panto script when I played Mrs Crusoe, at the White Rock Pavilion, in Hastings, in 1969, was signed on the fly-leaf by P. O'Toole. My researches revealed that Peter O'Toole had played the Dame in "Robinson and Crusoe", at Bristol Old Vic, a dozen years before. I liked the idea that I handled the same script as "El-Orens".

When "Laurence of Arabia" had its premiere Noel Coward was so taken with Peter O'Toole's physical appearance that he said it should have been re-named "Florence of Arabia".

* * * *

Mention of Peter O'Toole reminds me that Jo and I saw him, in startling form, in the West End hit, "Jeffrey Barnard Is Unwell". The real Jeffrey Barnard, due to his drink problem, did not drive. To overcome the problem of transportation he would post a letter to himself every day and then the next morning, when it was delivered, he would persuade the postman to give him a lift.

* * * *

My trombone teacher, in my teens, was Denis Wick, the lead trombonist with the City of Birmingham Symphony Orchestra. His playing was so phenomenal that Gordon Jacobs dedicated the first English trombone concerto to him. Wikipedia refers to him as "Britain's most influential trombonist of the twentieth century". Through no fault of Denis a description of yours truly would have been worded somewhat more modestly. ("Nominated as President of the Failed Trombonist's League", perhaps?)

* * * *

My trombone case used to double as a portable dressing room and I could fit everything into it except my suit. I must be the only person in Showbiz who would take their instrument into a shop to make sure that the shoes fitted the case.

Harking back to my band days – we were sometimes booked into the oddest of venues. One night, in the depth of winter, we found ourselves playing in a Nissen hut. Packing up afterwards a man came to congratulate us on a very pleasant evening only spoilt, in his words, by the drum solos. I retorted, "Hang on! We're a dance band, our drummer doesn't play any solos!" I thought for a second, "That was the hailstones on the corrugated roof!"

* * * *

We appeared at the Golden Butterfly nightclub, in Skegness, in cabaret with Eddie Calvert. By coincidence, the first record I ever bought, as a teenager, was his version of "Oh, Mein Papa". On the second night my pianist, Adrian Barnby, pleaded, "Don't let them put that green spotlight on me again. It makes me look like a demented elf."

* * * *

Due to an unusual mix-up, resulting in my regular musicians being on holiday, I finished up, for one night only, with a scratch band. Suddenly the sax player produced a violin and proceeded to play the most excruciating waltz ever. During the interval he came to me and complained, "Alton, will you have a word with that trumpeter please. He won't take his foot off my violin case."

* * * *

Combining my musical days with the book world – I saw a copy of my record "Alton Douglas Sings?" for sale on eBay. A reviewer had written, "Wherever you find a WH Smith shop in the Midlands there will always be an altar to Alton Douglas in beatific repose."

"GOING FOR THE JOCULAR"

A wise man once said that there was no such thing as an old joke as long as one person hadn't heard it. Some gags, no matter how often you have heard them, still make you smile. This little crop make me laugh out loud:

"I'm giving a party tomorrow and we're having some of those little wrinkly things on sticks."
    "Sausages?"
    "No – pensioners."

In our complex it's nearly all senior citizens. My wife went to a funeral last week and caught the wreath.

Asked to name a person who was gone but not forgotten someone replied, "Old Bill in Haberdashery. He's gone but not for cotton."

"The louder he spoke of his honour, the faster we counted the spoons." (Ralph Waldo Emerson)

"If you had a face like mine you'd punch me right on the nose and I'm the fella to do it." (Stan Laurel)

A dishevelled, scruffy-looking man walked into a chemist:
    "A bottle of methylated spirits, please."
    "No, I'm sorry."
    "Why not?"
    "I know what you'll do with it. You'll drink it."
    "I won't. I'm a roofer working next door and I've spilt some paint on the tiles. I need to clean them up before the owner sees the mess."
    "But you're a tramp."
    "I may look like one but I'm not going to get up on a roof in my best suit, am I?"
    "Oh, of course not. I do apologise. Here you are, Sir."
    "Thank you ———— haven't you got a cold one?"

Bertie Green, my manager when I was a comedian, in 1968, has appeared in our books before. He was the owner of London's Astor Club and, like a lot of Jewish people, was a lover of Jewish humour – a passion we both shared. I used to jot down his stories:

Two fellows walking along in the snow with their hands in their pockets:
> Abie: "Why don't you say something?"
> Morrie: "Freeze your own hands!"

The phone rings and Hymie picks it up:
> "Hallo."
> "Hymie, is that you?"
> "It's me."
> "Are you sure? I don't recognise the voice?"
> "I don't do impressions. It's me."
> "Are you positive?"
> "Yes. I've told you three times."
> "Oh, great. This is Solly. Can you lend me some money?"
> (Long pause) "I'll ask him when he comes in."

Bertie maintained his cousin was the meanest man he knew. He told me that he went to his house for a meal and caught him counting the salt.

The cousin and his wife didn't get on. Every morning he had a three minute egg and she had a five minute argument.

Something had always happened to Bertie (according to him) on his way to work. One particular morning he said that he had been stopped in the street by a poor relation:
> "Can you spare a pound for a coffee?"
> "Coffee is more than a pound these days."
> "So, who buys retail?"

AS YOU WRITE IT

As Shakespeare ferreted away
At sonnet and dramatic play,
His wife said, "I appreciate
The effort you've put in of late.

You've worked your brain-box to the bone
And I'm an awful shrew to moan;
But writing's just got out of hand
And Will, I just don't understand.

So, let's go back a bit in time -
Whoever mentioned prose or rhyme?
I asked you, when I broke my wrist,
To simply write a shopping list!"

(Published in the Daily Mail, 3rd October 2012)

HOW I LEARNED TO LOVE OGDEN NASH

When all the worthwhile rhymes are hogged then
Bet your life they're hogged by Ogden.
As English proved unsatisfactory
He built himself a wordsmith's factory.
So read his poems, get the hang, which
Should improve your use of langwhich.

"GULLIBLE'S TRAVELS"

I sat next to heavyweight boxing champion, Henry Cooper (one-time opponent of Cassius Clay) at a dinner in Bristol and he told a lovely story. He was driving along in pouring rain and the traffic lights suddenly turned to red. Henry slammed his brakes on and a cyclist behind ran into him. He got out to find, to put it mildly, an extremely irate man sparring up to him. Henry's identical twin, George, got out of the car followed by their manager, another man-mountain, Jim Wicks. They stood around the cyclist who was about 7 stone wringing wet and clenching his fists and yelling at Henry, "Oh, you've gone all bold now you've got your mates with you!"

✳   ✳   ✳   ✳

Phil Drabble was a Black Country author and television presenter. He was a solidly built man with a florid complexion that somehow seemed to give him a permanently angry look. As he stopped at a T junction another car drove into the back of him. He got out, confronted the driver and then, in the sweetest possible manner asked, "How do you normally stop when I'm not here?"

✳   ✳   ✳   ✳

Jack Lester, the Birmingham comic/clown, was being driven to a booking by a friend. Unfortunately, they met an American serviceman who was travelling around the island the wrong way. Smash! The police came to interview the drivers and one of them asked Jack, "Well, sir, you're a witness to this. We'll need your details. Name?" "John Lennon." His friend muttered, "Jack, don't mess about. Officer, this is Jack Lester, he's a comedian." "I'll ask you again, sir. Name?" "John Lennon." By then his friend was panicking "Jack, you'll lose me my licence. Tell him your real name." "John Lennon!"

And it was.

"PURE HAPPENSTANCE"

In my tenure with the band of the 5th Royal Inniskilling Dragoon Guards I developed quite a wide trombone vibrato. The result, I guess, of being continually jumped upon from a great height by Band Sgt Major McCoig (my fault, I'm sure, no one could have described me as a good soldier). I was able to console myself when I read the story of the Dorsey brothers and found that Jimmy had exactly the same problem, due to the constant arguments with Tommy. It was considered a virtue, however, because his alto playing became one of his band's most identifiable sounds.

* * * *

During my residency as comedian/compere at the Best Cellar, in Leicester Square, I happened to be passing the stage door of The Talk Of The Town when I heard the sound of a trombone. I asked the doorkeeper who it was and he told me that film musical comedy star, Dan Dailey ("Give My Regards To Broadway", "There's No Business Like Show Business", etc.) was going through his band call and that he finished his act on the instrument. I thought then that it was quite a coincidence that we were performing only a short distance from each other every night and both rounding off our acts in much the same way.

It also left me to reflect on two other comics who were trombonists – our own Jimmy Edwards and Jerry Colonna (who toured overseas in shows for the troops with Bob Hope). The other odd "happenstance" is that both of them had handlebar moustaches.

* * * *

Our webmaster, Ken, as a Glasgow community councillor, was invited to the Queen's Garden Party in Edinburgh. The invitation was for Ken and a companion and he chose to take his friend, Linda. The Palace asked for the names of the guests well in advance. Imagine the expressions on the faces of the Buckingham Palace officials when they discovered that their surnames were Windsor and Marquis!

Chatting to a lady in our local hospice shop she recommended a gardener to me. This has led to several years, up to the present, of friendship with Dave Kilner. The coincidence is that Dave had been a professional artiste with a vocal/guitar duo called, "Heartbeat Harmony".

A couple of members of his family had careers that fascinated me, being county cricketers. His grandad, Norman Kilner, played for Warwickshire and Yorkshire and his great-uncle, Roy Kilner, not only played for Yorkshire but made 11 Test appearances. He was so highly thought of that when he died in 1928, 100,000 people lined the funeral route.

* * * *

When we were compiling our book "Memories of Birmingham" in my quest for material I had to visit the Edgbaston Golf Club. The secretary said, "You'll want our steward, Mr Dollery". I went cold all over – Tom Dollery had been my cricketing idol throughout my young years. In a wonderful hour together he reminded me that it was through his efforts that the practice of amateurs and professionals using separate changing rooms and walking onto the pitch through different gates came to an end. He also told me that, as captain of Warwickshire C.C.C. he discovered, just before an important away match, a lot of the players had been out drinking. He then made sure that they were called an hour earlier than expected the next morning. When they arrived at the assembly point they found that there was no coach. He marched the team the two miles to the opponents' ground.

* * * *

Another great childhood hero, from my Saturday morning cinema visits, was Johnny Mack Brown. Thirty years later I was invited to a Western convention at the M & B Sports Club in Smethwick. I found myself shaking hands with the guest of honour – one of his daughters.

My Glaswegian landlady, Mrs Skilling, told me that, "Russ Conway had your room last week," I said, "By the feel of the mattress he's still there."

Shortly afterwards Russ and I did a show together, in Chester. Looking very nervous he confided in me, "This is the very first time I've ever done a cabaret." His companion muttered, "He says that every night."

✳ ✳ ✳ ✳

The flat I rented for the season, in Blackpool, had been occupied the previous year by John Stokes, the bass player with The Bachelors. Sometime later I did a tour with them.

My landlady at the time, said to me, "Nice bit of Parkin?" I replied, "I always try and park carefully." She retorted, "Parkin! Parkin! Do you want a piece of Parkin?" It's a Northern gingerbread cake.

✳ ✳ ✳ ✳

The Pete Price Combo backed me for two summer seasons in Blackpool. Three of the musicians were named Pete and the bandleader who eventually took over from them was John Peate.

My family share Pete Price's surname.

✳ ✳ ✳ ✳

I was born on the 22nd January, a distinction I share with a number of other people including: Sir John Hurt, Viscount St Alban Francis Bacon, Sir Walter Raleigh and Lord Byron.

On that day the No.1 film was "Happy Landing" and the No.1 record was Artie Shaw's "Begin The Beguine". I couldn't ask for anything more appropriate. I'm not prepared to discuss the aptness, or otherwise, of Jo's "birth film" – it was "Wee Willie Winkie".

"THE VIEW FROM THE BRIDGE"
(OR "WHERE MY SPECTACLES HAVE RESTED")

Autobiography	–	Life story written by the least appropriate person.
Bullock	–	Neither one thing or the other.
Committee	–	A group of people chosen for their determination to maintain a decision-free zone.
Dead Cert	–	Tenth finisher in a nine horse race.
Enterprising	–	Burglar's favourite method of gaining admittance.
Filibuster	–	A stallion.
Ghost	–	Indefinite article.
Hairy Coms	–	Prince Charles' greeting on seeing an old friend.
iPad	–	My home.
Juggernaut	–	Empty vessel.
Kick Boxer	–	Outlawed tactic for those involved in the noble art.
Lucky	–	Acquiring good fortune. Rather me than you.
Money Order	–	Instruction. Typified by: "Have the exact fare ready."
Numero Uno	–	Too good to be two.

Outpouring	–	Result of a novice wine waiter with an unsteady hand.
Plaintiff	–	A simple argument.
Quintessential	–	Five times as important.
Rear-view Mirror	–	Newspaper back number.
Stretch Marks	–	German budgetary requirement.
Triangle	–	A musical instrument for the non-musical. Consists of a metal bar bent into a three-sided shape and beaten with a metal stick (it has been suggested that the player should receive the same treatment).
Unprintable	–	Don't know. Never seen it in print.
VAT	–	Value added tax. Contradiction in terms for the payee.
Workforce	–	Hard-hearted members of the Employment Office.
Xenophobia	–	Fear of foreign-sounding words beginning with X.
Yo? (or Yow?)	–	Expression of surprise uttered by a Black Country person confronted by an unexpected visitor.
Zoot Suit	–	Male clothing, particularly popular in the 40s. Designed more for the comic than the straight man.

THANKS FOR NOTHING

At Xmas a dozy inventor
Sent his girlfriend a gift with no centre.
With no front and no back
And no sides to unpack
She can't open the present he's sent her.

EH?

A contrary old man from Hong Kong
Had argued a point for so long,
That they gave him his way
But he begged, "If you stay,
Then I think you'll find out that I'm wrong."

OFFICIAL'S VERDICT

In football the referee's seen
By 22 players as mean.
To the crowd it's his fate
To be someone they hate.
(When he gets home his wife isn't keen.)

SING UP!

A wonderful singer named Keith
Hits high notes and those underneath,
But because he's so old
(Though his voice is pure gold)
It won't travel as far as his teeth.

"OFF SCREEN"

I expect, like me, you have always enjoyed unexpected tales about film actors:

Rod Cameron: Canadian-born star of many B Westerns divorced his wife and married his mother-in-law. The director, William Withey, said that it was the bravest act he had ever heard of.

＊　＊　＊　＊

George Montgomery: He starred in such films as "Orchestra Wives", "China Girl" and "Satan's Harvest", married the singer, Dinah Shore, and went on to become a successful painter and sculptor. In 1963 his housekeeper was charged with attempting to murder him.

＊　＊　＊　＊

Lee Marvin: Best remembered for his roles in "The Dirty Dozen", "Cat Balou" and "The Man Who Shot Liberty Valance", he also had a hit record with the song, "I Was Born Under A Wandering Star", from "Paint Your Wagon". Despite all his days of stardom he valued his war service most highly. His headstone bears the inscription, "Lee Marvin PFC (Private First Class) US Marine Corps World War II."

＊　＊　＊　＊

George Tobias: A character actor. I imagine he is known to most of us as Cy Schribman, the man who financed the orchestra in "The Glenn Miller Story". When he died, in 1980, the hearse containing his body was stolen on the way to the mortuary. It was abandoned a mile down the road when the thieves realised they were not the only occupants.

During the Second World War, glamorous, Vienna-born actress, Hedy Lamarr, and her business partner, George Antheil, invented a communications system for radio-guided torpedoes. It eventually became a constituent part of Wi-Fi and Bluetooth technology.

"MAY THE FORCES BE WITH YOU"

During my stint, with the band of the 5th Royal Inniskilling Dragoon Guards, the Officer in charge of the band, left the regiment. I had the task of making a short speech and presenting him with a leaving gift. Afterwards, at the reception, obviously aware that I was a lowly bandsman, he asked me, "Why did they choose you to make the presentation?" I replied, displaying my usual rare gift for diplomacy, "We drew lots and I lost."

✳   ✳   ✳   ✳

One of my friends, in the band, was a very fine trombonist, the Salvationist, Bryan Summerfield. He left the band for a year to study at Kneller Hall. On arrival there he found that his tutor was a civilian musician from the London Symphony Orchestra. He gave Bryan a test piece to play in order to assess his ability. Bryan played, as he thought, quite well. The teacher looked at him long and hard and then said, "I think I'll put the kettle on."

✳   ✳   ✳   ✳

RSM Brittain had the most powerful voice in the British Army. It was rumoured that when he bellowed a command, in Aldershot, recruits in Catterick snapped to attention.

✳   ✳   ✳   ✳

Dennis Moore tells of a friend who was a Master Carpenter. After a delayed National Service call-up he was told that, despite his qualifications, he would still have to undergo the usual army tests. He then found himself in the Catering Corps. He quizzed the sergeant in charge of the cookhouse, "I can't understand it? How did I get from being a Master Carpenter to becoming a cook?" The sergeant replied, "Look at your results." He did and the comment was, "Joint well done."

Alec Owen's uncle, James, joined the Army, much against his better judgement, and was sent to be kitted out. After the basic equipment he was handed a rifle. The exchange then went as follows:

"What's this for, Sergeant?"

"It's for killing Germans."

"Well, I shan't need that then."

"Why not?"

"I'm not argumentative."

* * * *

A friend of my publisher, Alan Brewin, joined the 4th Hussars. Although, only a National Serviceman, he decided that he would like to become an Officer. An application was made and he found himself standing in front of his Commanding Officer:

"So, you want to be an Officer, eh? Tell me a bit about yourself. Any hobbies or anything like that?"

"Well, Sir, I did once ride across France."

"Rode across France did you? Did you hear that, Adjutant? My God? What sort of horse had you got?"

"Oh, no Sir, it was on my bike."

"On a bike? On a bike? Adjutant put this man down for an NCO's course!"

* * * *

Alan had, in his own squad, a fellow-recruit whose name was John Thomas Smaller. Can you imagine being on parade for the first roll call when the Sergeant calls out, "Smaller: John Thomas"?

* * * *

An old school friend, a Junior Karate Champion, was recruited into the Navy. On one of his leaves I asked him how he was getting on, "Not bad at all except that the first time I saluted I nearly killed myself."

Neil Allen was called up into the Royal Air Force:

"I qualified as an L.A.C. Radio Telephony Operator working in Air Traffic Control and as part of a 24 hour distress watch I was situated in a decrepit vehicle, parked in a farmer's field, a few hundred yards from the end of the runway.

One afternoon we were experiencing the mother and father of all thunderstorms and the poor old vehicle gave up. Water starting pouring in. I was getting soaked and elected to put my uniform into a cupboard and work in my PT shorts.

Suddenly a pilot's voice called for a bearing, followed by several more requests until he called that he could see the runway.

Some minutes later I heard the unsuppressed ignition of the Air Traffic Control jeep in my headphones and was horrified to see, striding towards the van, none other than the A.O.C., Air Commodore Forrow, CB, OBE. He was the pilot and had come to thank me for the bearings! The expression on his face when he saw this near naked, bedraggled airman opening the rear doors were memorable. All I could think of saying was, 'Sorry, Sir, I think we've got a leak'!"

✳   ✳   ✳   ✳

Officer: "Can you change a five pound note, please?"
Airman: "Yes, mate."
Officer: "Mate? That's no way to answer an Officer! Try again. Can you change a five pound note, please?"
Airman: "No, SIR!"

✳   ✳   ✳   ✳

Let us leave the final word on the military to the Duke of Wellington. During the Napoleonic Wars he said, of his own men, "I don't know what effect these men will have on the enemy, but by God, they frighten me!"

"IT'S JUST NOT CRICKET"

Apart from Showbiz, reading and jazz, my other great love has always been cricket. However, I am often reminded that it can be a very cruel sport. Someone once said that most political lives end in tears and that could equally apply to many sporting lives. It seems to me that the attainment of perfection is always a sliver away from human grasp, or is it best explained as "the blemish that makes perfection bearable"?

Mark Boucher: South African wicketkeeper for 15 years, he had to retire after an eye injury in 2012. He had 998 international dismissals to his credit.

❋　❋　❋　❋

Jim Laker: In the Ashes match, at Old Trafford, the Englishman took 19 wickets for 90 runs. One short of a majority.

❋　❋　❋　❋

Norman Kilner: As I have mentioned before, in his career he played for Yorkshire and Warwickshire. His combined tally of county appearances was 399.

❋　❋　❋　❋

Don Bradman: The Australian, still considered, by most of us, to be the greatest batsman ever, was out for 0 in his last Test. If he had scored 4 more runs his Test average would have been 100 and he would have made 7,000 runs in Tests.

❋　❋　❋　❋

Eric Hollies: Another great hero of mine. It was Eric who dismissed The Don in his last Test match for a duck. This superb Warwickshire slow bowler must also have been one of the most inept batsman ever to play county cricket. Out of a mixture of hilarity and affection we would applaud him all the way to the wicket. After one innings of 7 he received a standing ovation.

"STICKING TO THE BRIEF"

I get very annoyed at the misspelling of artistes' names. In the last week I have seen Glen Miller and Cliff Richards! It seems a simple courtesy to check before committing a name to print. I was once billed as "Aileen Douglas".

✳   ✳   ✳   ✳

After my act, in a club, two young girls said, "We'd like to buy you a drink." Preening myself I walked over to the bar to hear, "What would you like, Grandad?"

✳   ✳   ✳   ✳

Talk about giving with one hand and taking with the other – I bumped into a man, in the centre of Birmingham, who recognised me, "I remember seeing you in a late night revue about 40 years ago. I can still picture your outfit now. You wore a jacket I would have killed to own," he hesitated, "But I wouldn't have been seen dead in those trousers."

✳   ✳   ✳   ✳

I compered the stage version of the TV hit series "Stars and Garters". The guest star was the comedian and character actor, Harold Berens. Although born in Glasgow, Harold was generally thought of as a Jewish Cockney. Walking around one town he stopped and indicating a row of shops cried, "Jacoby! Goldsmith! Samuels! Cor stone me, this place is full of five by twos."

He had been quite a big name in the days of variety and as a member of the panel of the radio programme "Ignorance Is Bliss" but, with the advent of cabaret, his star had waned. Ironically, not being a big eater himself, he spotted the burgeoning supermarkets and invested what money he had in several of them. He quickly regained his former wealth.

When I appeared at the London Palladium, in 1974, it was a variety bill which included Matt Monro, Max Wall and the jazz pianist, Bill McGuffie. Bill only played a couple of numbers but to me they were pure magic. Afterwards we talked about his time with the Benny Goodman Orchestra. He said that when Benny glared at anyone (it was known as "The Ray") even the toughest musicians would quake.

One day they had to rehearse the small group at Benny's house. It was a very cold winter and they realised that the central heating was not on. One of the band said, "Benny, it's very cold in here." Benny replied, "So it is. I'll do something about that!" He left the room and came back a few minutes later wearing a pullover.

* * * *

My friend, Keith Ackrill, because of his regular TV appearances, found himself with a fan. Somehow she obtained his home phone number and would ring him regularly for a chat. One night she confided in him, "We've bought a cat and to remind us of you we've called him 'Keith'. We're taking him tomorrow to have him neutered."

* * * *

One of Keith's jobs, at that time, was to read the late night news on BBC 1. One evening he was in his future wife's flat when a man from the Electricity Board turned up. He saw Keith and said, "Don't I know you from somewhere?" Keith didn't want to say, "You've probably seen me on television", because it would have seemed big-headed. So, they went through where they were born, the schools they went to, the youth clubs they might have joined, but nothing matched. Finally, the man said, "Hang on, are you something to do with the BBC?" Keith said he was. "Do you read the news last thing at night?" Keith said he did. "Ah!" The man was thrilled, "You're the bloke! Whenever you come on my wife always says to me, 'Come on Harry, come and watch, this is the bloke who always gets it wrong!' "

From the Dept. of the Inexplicable comes this word for word conversation I had with a customer in a bookshop:

"Our family has put a lot of money in your pocket."

"Why, do they buy all our books?"

"No, we borrow them from the library."

"I think you'd be very surprised if you knew how little authors make from library borrowings."

"You make a lot more from them than my husband."

"Is he an author then?"

"No, he's a bus driver."

* * * *

I overheard a conversation, in another bookshop, between a customer and an elderly assistant:

"I'm thinking of purchasing one of those Kindles for my wife. Are they easy to operate?"

"Oh, yes. She'll have no trouble at all. They're simplicity itself."

"I wonder if you'd mind showing me how they work."

"I'm afraid I can't do that, Sir."

"Why not?"

"I don't know how."

* * * *

One of our very first publications was "Celebrity Recipes" (a self-explanatory title if ever there was one). We wrote to several well-known people asking for their contributions. One morning I had a call from a voice I instantly recognised, "Mr Douglas, you can't possibly put in your book that Lord Longford likes beefburgers!"

Upon publication we sent a complimentary copy to everyone concerned. Fast forward another 30 years and I saw on the internet that someone was offering a copy for £75, including our original letter and a dedication that read, "Many thanks to Senator Edward Kennedy".

The Birmingham Mail published our first local book, "Birmingham at War", in 1982. After a few weeks I received a call to say, "Alton, we have had more of your books stolen, from the loading bay, than anything else in the company's history." To this day I am not sure if it was a compliment or not?

* * * *

We were signing copies of "Memories of Dudley" at the local branch of WH Smith. Covers and photographs from the book were festooned all over the walls behind us. A lady approached us and asked, "Are there any pictures of Dudley in this book?" I looked at her, indicated the surroundings and, with just a hint of sarcasm, replied, "No, I'm sorry we couldn't find any so we put Walsall photos in instead." She grabbed a book and, throwing it across the table, yelled at me, "Well, it's no effing good to me then!"

* * * *

A conversation with a man in Foster's Garden Centre, near Lichfield, has always intrigued me. He opened with:

"I've been very disappointed with your local books over the years."

"Why is that?"

"You've never featured a picture of my family's shop in the Bull Ring."

"When did you send me one?"

"I haven't sent you one."

"Why is that?"

"I haven't got one."

"Well, neither have I."

He struggled with that for a moment and then expostulated: "Why not?"

"I suppose, if your family didn't think that it was important to take a photograph, why would anyone else?"

Again he battled with the thought before storming off with an indignant exit line:

"That sounds very selfish to me!"

A lady approached me clicking her fingers, "I'm trying to remember where I know you from. You're —-?" Being helpful, I said, "I'm Alton Douglas." She looked very embarrassed so I tried to help again, "Don't worry. I often have the same problem." She looked startled, "Why? Can't you remember your name?"

✳   ✳   ✳   ✳

We were having new windows fitted and the workman was talking about his experience the week before, "The customer said she'd never seen her old windows as clean and sparkling as the new ones. I told her to hang on a sec until we'd put the glass in."

✳   ✳   ✳   ✳

I am sure that, like us, you are always hospitable towards workmen – "Tea? Coffee?" One of our neighbours is definitely not. The workman had been in the house since early morning and completely ignored. Around mid-afternoon he said to her, "I wonder if you could spare me a mug of water, please?" "No," she replied sharply, "I do not supply workmen with refreshments." He glared at her, "I need to make some paste."

✳   ✳   ✳   ✳

Fed up with all those calls canvassing you to buy anything from double-glazing to drip-dry concrete? This could be the answer:

"Hello, could I speak to the lady of the house?"

"Certainly. Can I tell her what it is about?"

"I'm sorry. I'm afraid I'm not allowed to give you that information under the Data Protection Act. Is she there, please?"

"I'm sorry. I'm afraid I'm not allowed to give you that information under the Data Protection Act."

By popular request a few more comments about artistes that could have been made by their arch enemy, the Working Men's Club Entertainment Secretary:

We had to cancel the accordionist due to the squeeze.

The dancers told me that they had been choreographed but I assured them that no one had noticed.

There were complaints from members when the singer asked for the jukebox to be switched off during her act.

A friend of mine summed it up when he said, "You don't have to be deaf to hear she's out of tune."

The Weoley Castle Chippendales are very popular but my wife thought they left a lot to be desired.

They were followed by a two minute silence to celebrate the death of Tom our oldest living member.

I have always enjoyed Valentino and His Doves but it was just unfortunate that they were booked on the same night as the local rifle team.

The audience did not like the operatic tenor. He sang some German lieder but our members refused to sing along with him.

The beat group on Saturday were so loud that my brother-in-law, who is stone-deaf, turned his hearing aid off and he could still hear them.

The agent said that the strongman could not fit us in because he was solidly booked for the weak.

I thought the end of his act was very funny. Singing "Rawhide" he repeatedly banged himself over the head with a tin tray. Unfortunately, he was unable to do a second spot due to being unconscious.

I warned him that sword swallowing would not go down well in our club.

You could not compere him with our old compare. It was like cork and cheese.

The members liked the juggling of Melia and her Indian clubs. It was such a shame that the drummer chose the climax of her act to lean forward to get a better view.

The escapologist did all he could to wriggle out of his contract.

It was a hard job persuading her to play "The Trumpet Voluntary".

The senior citizens' Xmas party was a great success although I don't think the Limbo Dancing Competition was such a good idea.

There was no need for him to be so rude when I asked how many were in the quartet.

The Punch and Judy man has cancelled his booking because of the violence.

Our new resident duo entertained us on Saturday. Some of our regulars said that they had never heard anything like it.

The coach, carrying the choir, arrived an hour late. They blamed it on the conductor. I never knew that private coaches had a conductor.

In my early days, as a comedian, I arrived at a typically grotty club to be met by the Entertainment Secretary, "How do you want introducing?" "Just say, 'Ladies and gentleman, Alton Douglas!' That'll do." He said, "Oh! No – no – the agent's changed the act again. He's always doing that to us. Do you mind if I introduce you as the act we've got billed this week?" I looked at him disbelievingly, "I don't suppose it matters how you introduce me." So that night I was Ted Scott.

Afterwards a man grabbed hold of me, "Hey, you were great, Ted. Far better than the bloke we had last week." I said, "Thank you, who was that?" He thought, for what seemed like an eternity, "I can't remember his name – yes, I can – Alton Douglas!"

ALTON'S BOOKS – STILL IN PRINT !

"ENTERTAINING THOUGHTS"
"LAUGHS IN THE RIGHT PLACE"
"I FORGOT TO TELL YOU"
"A LOAD OF NONSENSE!"
"SHOCKING NONSENSE!"
"THE ORIGINAL ALTON DOUGLAS"
"BIRMINGHAM: 1900 TO 1970"
"BIRMINGHAM IN THE THIRTIES"
"BIRMINGHAM: THE THIRTIES REVISITED"
"BIRMINGHAM: BACK TO THE FORTIES"
"BIRMINGHAM IN THE FORTIES"
"BIRMINGHAM: BACK TO THE FIFTIES"
"BIRMINGHAM IN THE FIFTIES VOL 1"
"BIRMINGHAM IN THE FIFTIES VOL 2"
"BIRMINGHAM: MORE OF THE FIFTIES!"
"BIRMINGHAM: THE FIFTIES REVISITED"
"BIRMINGHAM: BACK TO THE SIXTIES"
"BIRMINGHAM IN THE SIXTIES VOL 1"
"BIRMINGHAM: MORE OF THE SIXTIES"
"BIRMINGHAM: THE SIXTIES REVISITED"
"BIRMINGHAM: BACK TO THE SEVENTIES"
"BIRMINGHAM IN THE SEVENTIES"
"BIRMINGHAM IN THE 70s AND 80s"
"THE BIRMINGHAM SCRAPBOOK VOL 1"
"THE BIRMINGHAM SCRAPBOOK VOL 2"
"BIRMINGHAM SHOPS"
"BIRMINGHAM AT WAR VOL 1"
"BIRMINGHAM AT WORK"
"MEMORIES OF THE BLACK COUNTRY"
"MEMORIES OF DUDLEY"
"MEMORIES OF WEST BROMWICH"
"COVENTRY: A CENTURY OF NEWS"
"COVENTRY AT WAR"
"MEMORIES OF COVENTRY"
"MEMORIES OF STRATFORD-UPON-AVON"

Contact leading booksellers or for ORDER FORM please write to:
Alton Douglas, c/o Brewin Books Ltd.,
Doric House, 56 Alcester Road, Studley, Warwickshire, B80 7LG.
www.altondouglas.co.uk